Sky Burial

Books by Dana Levin

Sky Burial

Wedding Day

In the Surgical Theatre

Sky Burial

DANA LEVIN

COPPER CANYON PRESS
PORT TOWNSEND, WASHINGTON

Copyright 2011 by Dana Levin

Printed in the United States of America

Cover art: Linda Connor, *April 16, 1893*. Gold toned contact print, 14 x 17 inches. Courtesy of Photo Eye Gallery. © Linda Connor and Regents of the University of California, Lick Observatory's Mt. Hamilton Plate Archive.

Copper Canyon Press is in residence at Fort Worden State Park in Port Townsend, Washington, under the auspices of Centrum. Centrum is a gathering place for artists and creative thinkers from around the world, students of all ages and backgrounds, and audiences seeking extraordinary cultural enrichment.

LIBRARY OF CONGRESS CATALOGING-IN-PUBLICATION DATA
Levin, Dana.
 Sky burial / Dana Levin.
    p. cm.
ISBN 978-1-55659-332-1 (pbk. : alk. paper)
I. Title.
PS3562.E88953S58 2011
811´.54—dc22

                              2010038351

98765432 FIRST PRINTING

COPPER CANYON PRESS
Post Office Box 271
Port Townsend, Washington 98368
www.coppercanyonpress.org

Acknowledgments

While writing this book I was grateful to have the insights of many friends and fellow writers. Deepest gratitude to Michael Wiegers and Copper Canyon Press; and to Matt Donovan, Dan George, Louise Glück, and G.C. Waldrep.

Thanks also to the Rona Jaffe, Whiting, and Guggenheim foundations, which afforded me time and encouragement; as well as to the editors who published these poems (some in earlier forms) in these journals:

Alhambra Poetry Calendar 2009: "Ichor."

The American Poetry Review: "Corpse Pose," "Ghosts That Need Reminding," "Letter to GC," "The Mentor," "Pure Land," "White Tara."

Connotations Press: An Online Artifact: "Among the Living."

Gulf Coast: "Augur."

The Iowa Review: "Spring."

The Kenyon Review: "Zozo-ji."

Kenyon Review Online: "Five Skull Diadem."

Memorious: "The Water."

The Paris Review: "In Honor of Xipe," "Sibylline," *"Therefore Direct Your Feelings, Senses, Reason, Thoughts Upon This Stone Alone,"* "This from That."

Pasatiempo: "Art Sutra."

Perihelion: "The Charisma of the Doctor," "Judd Boxes."

Ploughshares: "Her Dream."

Poetry: "Ichor," "Pyro," "Refuge Field," "School of Flesh."

Poetry Daily: "Spring," "Sun Sutra," "Zozo-ji."

Poets.org (Academy of American Poets): "Styx."

Salmagundi: "Cathartes Aura," "Bardo."

Witness: "Sun Sutra."

for Caryn

CONTENTS

Sky Burial

AUGUR

Hawk perched low on a hedge of vine.

On hunt for what hid
     in the tangle.

The small citizens, mouse and gopher.

Body of Ra the hawk signified.

In the symbol book, which I opened after climbing the stairs,
     after the hawk fanned out its banded tail like I should

     pick a card—

The book was a prisoner of my ardor for the dark—through it I stalked,
     a seeker.

It was a character out of a Victorian novel—*Symbol Book,* an
     imbecile, a Dutch inventor.

Saying, You must bow
     to the Hippogriff (half raptor, half horse), it must

     lower its head to your hand.

Halcón Pradeño. Mexicano. Come to me for my winter ground.

According to Whatbird.com.

Hawk perched low on a hedge of vine. Going
     heel to toe, so as not to startle.

Cloud unhooding *body of Ra* a pale pearl of winter sun—

Renaissance printers
     often stamped their wares with a hooded falcon,

     emblem of the dungeoned seer.

That "hope for light" the darkened nourish.

Closed books, *post tenebras spero lucem* along the spine—

I found the phrase in the Office for the Dead, in the Latin Vulgate:
     after darkness I hope for light—

Then: *hell is my house, and in darkness I have made my bed*—

I thought of my father and mother and sister being dead, I was so sick
     of feeling anything about it—

The hood stood for hope of liberty.

Of wanting to swoop and soar over enormous swells,
     as in my dream.

I hovered high, I could see the mammals in the raucous waters, their slick
     skins
of danger and wonder.

My soul hath thirsted, the Vulgate said, *He hath put a new song
     into my mouth.*

The hawk appeared. Unhooded.
     An auspice, from *auspex, avispex,* "one who looks at birds"—

I'd been wanting to know if it was all right to live.

An ascensional symbol on every level, the symbol book said.

Body of Ra. Solar victory. If one can believe the book
of symbols.

GHOSTS THAT NEED REMINDING

Through shattered glass and sheeted furniture, chicken wire and piled dishes, sheared-off doors stacked five to a wall, you're walking like cripples. Toward a dirty window, obstructed by stacks of chairs.

And once you move them, one by one, palm circles through the grime and cup your hands round your faces, finally able to see through—

Charged night. Sheet-flashes of green, threaded with sparks, the pale orange pan of the moon—

Finally, what turns the wheel: the moon ghosting a hole through a rainbow, the rainbow's rage to efface the moon, which the moon sails through slow as a ship, in the shape of a cross-legged Buddha...

Lotus-folded, a figurine. The kind you once found in the Chinatown markets, for a dollar and a dime—

Saying, You're dying, you're dead. You can withdraw from this orbit of mirrors.

CATHARTES AURA

sky burial

Sound of ripping paper through the corridor of joys.

Someone keeps pushing the needle
       from the record, someone fallen in mid-song—

Behold.

Golden Purifier. Opening its black wings to the sun.

        —

They took you in an ambulance even though you were dead,
they took you

and my sister said

Why are you saving her if she is dead?

       shey   shey—

Curve of sky a crescent blade.

Vultures wheeling
       on thermal parapets, *shunyata,*

       void that flays—

Yak butter,

      barley flour and tea: you watch him

      make the paste.

—

Hanks of hair along the gully's seam.

Hank of hair in the butcher's hand, he'll scrape
      the crown-door clean—

Help him now. Drag her over to the flat rock,
      it's porous, it will drink

      the stain—

Tie to your waist a burlap sack, fit to your head an old
      surgical cap, wipe

      his flay-blade clean.

—

What is the body but a bag of alms

for the Infection-Eaters, who will cleanse the corpse to the bone—

Sever her arm.

Pound it
        with the back of an ax, it's the pulp that sets

        the paste—

Human barley cakes.

Until

        —

she is the jellied wealth they dive for, heads
        featherless and slick—

He's waving them away with a long white stick, your
        ritual-butcher friend.

You must finish, you must
        sever her head—

What is an arm but an alm.

        —

Sound of ripping paper through the corridor of joys.

Someone pushing the needle
        from the record, someone falling in mid-song—

There is a law.

That one must put color
      to the lips of the dead—

      file them in the ground under a name—

Smash the skull.

For the eaters, who will bear the used body away.

Letter to GC

I say most sincerely and desperately, HAPPY NEW YEAR!
Having rowed a little farther away from the cliff
Which is my kind of religion
Adrift in the darkness but readying oars
How can there be too many stars and hands, I ask you

—

I would be disingenuous if I said "being understood" is not important to me
Between the ceiling of private dream and the floor of public speech
Between the coin and the hand it crosses
Mercantilists' and governors' and preachers' alike
The imagination and its products so often rebuff purpose
And some of us don't like it, and want to make it mean
I would never shoot you, even if you were the only meat around

—

Anyway, snow-bound sounds gorgeous and inconvenient
Like the idea of ending on the rhyme of *psychics* and *clients*
Though I too privilege the "shiny"
And of course, I want to be approved of, so much
Despite the image I've been savoring, the one of the self-stitching wound
Yes, I want to write that self-healing wound poem, the one with
       cocoon closed up with thorns
We are getting such lovely flourishes from our poets
Fathomless opportunities for turning literacy into event

It's the drama of feeling we find such an aesthetic problem,
   these days

PURE LAND

Shedding-So-Glorious—
Buddha
        of the autumn djinns—

His Consort, Golden-
Sensation—

You'd brushed by chamisa. A
honey-palaced air—

As if a smell
could be a place, musk-heavy and gold,
        a glorious
Pure
        Land—

Who could breathe in it.

Who got to breathe
in it

without a body, dimmed
bulb
        of form—

Could the dead breathe,
scorched and bright,
        in a sun come

to scour the skin from each waiting face,
snip the lid from each
sleepless eye—saying *You*

who'd wanted to feel
the true burn,
who'd wanted not meat

but light—

You must settle
with your deck of flesh—

an antique notion, I know.

ICHOR

The father died and then the mother died.
  And you were so addicted

to not feeling them, you told no one about the clamp
  inside—

around the vena cava. Dam against the blood's
  trash—

But I've got you now. Trussed at the waist
  in a wooden chair,

odor of spice and
  oranges, clove-pierced, incandescent stores

  to light our lab's decor—

Here. I saved this just for you.
  Beetle-cleaned and sharp at the tip, the finger that shook

in your set face
  from the hand that smoothed your hair—

Make a fist.
  Wrap the tube round your fleshy arm, pull the black rubber

tight—
  will we finally

see the sludge of their accumulated mouths, *Ah,* you've said,
  how they poisoned me...

Pierce in

      with your mother's finger-bone, taste the slow up-well—

Sweet.

      Sweet. Surge ambrosial and clear—

A honey, an ichor.

      From those who waited long

      in your veins.

STYX

You put a bag around your head and walked into the river.
You

walked into the river with a bag around your head and you were
never dead,
   in your land of scythe and snow—

game on the banks of your
mental styx

for the double
audience

of smoke—

    —

You pressed a coin into his palm and stepped across the water.
You

stepped across the water with a hand on his arm and he was
silent and kind as you
   shoved off, toward the smoky coils

of the greek-seeming dead—
You'd been trying to sleep.

Found yourself here
in the mythocryptic land—

The river

—

had widened to a lake. You were anchored
in the shallow boat

by his faceless weight—
And on the green shore you could see their vapored

residue, how they could
smell it, those two: if you

—

slit your wrist you could make them speak.

Refuge Field

You have installed a voice that can soothe you: *agents*
of the eaten flesh, every body

a cocoon of change—

Puparium. The garden
a birthing house, sarcophagidae—

And green was so dark in the night-garden, in the garden's
gourd of air—

green's epitome
of green's peace, the beautiful inhuman

leg-music, crickets'
thrum—
a pulse

to build their houses by,
each
successive molt

a tent of skin
in which skin can grow, the metallic sheen
of their blue backs

as they hatch out, winged and mouthed—

Like in a charnel ground, you sit and see.

In one of the Eight Great
Cemeteries, you sit and see—

How the skull-grounds
          are ringed by flame, how they spread out under

a diamond tent, how the adepts
          pupate
among bones—

          saying *I who fear dying, I who fear
being dead—*

          Refuge field.

          See it now.

That assembly of sages you would have yourself
          build,
to hear the lineage
          from mouth to ear, encounter the truth-

          chain—

saying *Soft eaters, someone's children, who gives them
          refuge from want—*

Cynomyopsis cadaverina. On every tongue
          they feed.

AMONG THE LIVING

A young woman flops down at a table, asking loudly, "Is there pecan pie today?" Broken protocol: you're supposed to go up to the counter, place your order, wait for your food, and when it's ready, take it to your seat to eat. The cook says, "No, pecan-*cheese* today," and the woman at the table starts crying. You think, "Yes, she is crazy," and then she starts looking through the trash, calling out brightly, "I'm just looking for a piece of pie—" Everyone ignores her: the three older dykes next to you, the Albanians behind the counter, you with a fork in your blueberry pie, everyone watches her intently through the backs of their heads, foreheads homing in on her like radar, thinking, "Yes, she is crazy." She finds the potato salad in the container you threw away and draws it carefully out of the trash, she takes the croutons from the Caesar salad you'd ordered and pours them on top, she keeps jerking slightly, a spastic electricity in her head, neck, arms, legs—

You can't finish your pie. You get up and put on your coat, everyone watching you intently with their foreheads. You take your pie to her, say, "Do you want the rest of this? I can't eat any more—" And she nods her head shyly, looks up, then down, then up at your face, says, "I thought you had blue eyes," and you say, "No, they're brown," and she says, "My friend wanted to have purple eyes but something went wrong," and you say, "Really?" and throw your coffee in the trash, and she dives after it saying, "Oh, is that tea?" and you say, "Oh, I'm sorry," everyone ignoring you, listening to you, chins pressed to their chests, and she stops digging, squints up in wonder, says, "Your hair is streaming out in waves—"

and you know she means you are a person, a fact as blinding as the sun.

The Water

An astrologer told you: a glorious son and a darkening daughter, and there she was, our R, for the fourth time that dinner hour filling to the brim a tall plastic cup, then sweeping it full to the floor; the night you were dying (though no one knew), hurling cups of ice at each other until you gasped, doubled-over: you never missed a fight, drowned girls who yearned to talk to each other—

She was autistic, fifteen, a torment, and you were her mother: elephant-legged and kidneys failing, twenty liquid pounds in each thigh; R fills to the brim a tall plastic cup. The drowned speak through the water.

The Mentor

The Mentor was in town to give a lecture, he was staying in my apartment. Too sick to attend, his wife stayed behind and I to nurse her. That night, the Mentor still away, curled in pain, she crept to my room to sleep with me. Hunched in bed she cried and shook, and in the morning when I woke up she was dead. I cradled her dead body in misery, for now I had to tell the Mentor.

I tracked him to a diner and found him in a booth drinking coffee. He was jovial, began showing me a collection of organa: eggs, seashells, stones, pond water in jars—I grab his hand mid-flourish, say, "Have you seen your wife?" And he looks confused, something gassing his eyes, he says, "Is she gone?" getting upset, and then smiling, saying, "When she comes back, I don't think she'll come back as a person, I think she'll come back as her clothes—she loved them so, the threads, the dyes—" Then he is staring into a tin can full of water, murky water almost red, and I know this will be our science: mourning her.

PYRO

You're gonna strike the match—

You're gonna strike it—

Flame the bank up into pods
        of fire, be

        a masterhand—

        —

And someone said, Gasoline.

Someone said, We have to change the images
        inside their heads, said

Gasoline?

And motor oil, he bought at a mini-mart.

        —

And the cat said Don't
        even though it was dead
and the squirrel said Don't
and the little dog missing an eye and a leg
        even though they were dead, said

Don't Don't

but you did it anyway.

And someone said, That boy is sick—
And someone said, It was kind of pretty

        when you didn't know what it was from the road.

        —

Hours now, by the trashed banks, counting
        the colored
glass—

Brown for beer. Green
        for the fizzy water, clear
for anything and
        taillights smashed, cars mucked like
big cats
        trapped in tar, who
ate the flesh right off their legs, if they were
        lighter
they could hurry home, they could float
        on
home—

        killed cat dead at the end of your stick, who could
do that,
        shot in the head—

Like in the shows where the cop
cleans up his town,
           then the ambulance comes for the drowned.

           —

You felt bad, so you did it.

You thought it was pretty, so you
           did it again.

You felt charged and buoyant
           as you picked your way home

           to the blue-lit fatherless den—

So you did it again.

The BB-ed mutt, leg smashed, home-bum toasting you
           with his beer as you
dragged it
           to the sludgy bank, the match, the gas, the
pile of tires someone had dumped, *Were you*
           dumped? you had asked
after another one left, and she had

           slapped you,
and slapped—

You were an ambulance, you could see she had drowned—

Like in the shows where the warrior
        collects his dead and
brings them to the shore,
        to burn them
in their body-boats, release
        the spiritual

        —

smoke—

And the parents said,
        Didn't he have a house-key around his neck,
didn't he have a pager, an electrical tether
        to a list of chores and a stocked refrigerator—

And the teachers said Yes, but what
        were the images inside his head, they
see it and they make it
        be—

And you put it in a tire, your
        viking boat,
you set it on fire and it kept afloat
        as it sailed down the river—
to the heaven of not being
        here.

CORPSE POSE

I

The whole left side of my upper back seized so that I could
not feel the beat—only by pressing in one spot, nestled inside
the shoulder blade, could I feel anything in my *abandoned child
under the overpass, huddling in the drench of after-rain*—

—

Wondering what he thought about my life. As if being dead
meant he might be more

philosophical—

especially after his soul-debriefing before the Committee
of Transport—

—

Voice the distance you were inhabiting:

Peanut Butter Zig Zag Soy Delicious Ice Cream.

2

Only by lying in one spot could one keep the dead from becoming vapor.

> *rappeling*
> *into her navel with a rope—*

Even though there were spots you didn't like to visit: her hands, her breath, her thighs—

—

Then love went looking for death like a detective, a detective after a noble criminal

> *consorts of the same*
> *saffron robe—*

for the parents were lifted from love's pool.

—

Taking a rest from them being dead. Taking a rest from them being alive—

> *every grief a teacher*

in corpse pose on a yoga mat in front of the refrigerator.

SCHOOL OF FLESH

Blush for a cheek of stone.

Blush for the lips sewn tight with thread, no speech
for the dead
maker—

You've got the razor. You can make each suture
snap.

And watch the mouth
bloom up with foam,
as if he'd drowned himself in soap—

You lift the neck and let the head drop back.
The mouth yawns wide its prize—

White thrive.
The larval joy.
Hot in their gorge on the stew of balms,
a moist exhale—
as if there were a last breath, a taunt
coiling
into your inner ear, *Good Dog,* you dig your hands in,
up-cupping
the glossal
bed—
saying, Graduate
of the School of Flesh, Father Conspirator—
I will

bite the tongue from the corpse—

THE CHARISMA OF THE DOCTOR

Radiance dissolves like a bromide in the gut
which is why the food you eat hasn't killed you yet.

—meridians where the long needles go in
to turn some kind of dial—

I can see from that rash in your navel
that you've hooked your tube to the mother-drug.
Give up sugar and make room for God.

Five Skull Diadem

at the Los Angeles County Museum of Art

I

Because

you believe in your skin, you must

elect the knife.

Peel the hair, the scalp-skin down.
Bow to the fruit-bearing crown.

—

When someone asked Rinzai
to define the essence of Buddhist teaching, he

stepped from his chair and slapped
the questioner's face.

Dazed and ashamed I stood.

Before the fantastic monsters, flame-fringed,
speaking the mudra

soliloquies: Fear not, I bestow the boon
of a corpse-headed pike, to gut

your mind's
self-cherishing—

Look at them, my sister says.

     They want to clean out your head with a trowel.

—

    Necklaced with bloody, freshly-severed-head garland,
    your three eyes flash and bulge and dart about,
    your mouth gapes with sharp fangs gnashing,
    breath panting with poisonous snake vapors!

    Lord Yamantaka, terrible form that tames all evil—
    reverently, I bow!

      TSONG KHAPA'S PRAISE OF THE INNER YAMA

stenciled in white on a black wall.

2

The hook because he pulls (others to salvation).

The noose because he binds (to the perfect wisdom).

The lance, because he pierces false theories.

Intestines draped over his twenty-fourth arm to explain our essential
    situation.

3

Field trip: to
          Circle of Bliss—

Museum show where you stand in clumps
          before the Wrathful—

Lost in the mind's
          imprisoned winds, its many-headed forms.

A lot of people
          in the room back there, the one you've ignored:

          Realm of Compassionate Gods—

You preferred eyeballs and blood in the offering bowl.

My sight my life in holy
          demolition.

Your sister rhapsodic (an "enlightenment nectar!")
          about the room back there,

          where you had to take the scare quotes off—

Kindness. You needed
          a savage kind.

Yama yak-headed whirlwinding in flames
          into your trip with death—

Which was your trip with flesh.

You had to be
                dismembered—just to

                loosen your grip.

By so many means, so many dead, yet these gods were suggesting
                kindness—

For all of us would be torn

                        —

                asunder—

4

They weren't really gods, they were
                "emanations."

Your choice to cloud up with the monstrous ones
                if the gentle ones didn't

                inspire

your plasmatic breath, your mental
                exhalations.

5

Because you believe in your skin.

Because
          you swing with a flourish: pride, blame, want, etc.—

Elect the knife.

Cut the cap from your head, dig in
          to the mind's

          hard country—

Until blue skies and white peaks.

In photos
          along the exit hall, a "geography

          —

          of the soul"—

They forged a faith
          with death as a condition, those Buddhist

Himalayans.
          A red art under a black sky, where the stars

glittered sharp,
          where the stars hung

          —

       cold and high—

Bones for sale in the museum shop.

Skull chic in the land of plenty.

I had to shake my dream
       of I-am-I.

Art Sutra

to find a conduit to awakening that is not suffering—

> *in the shiver of one candle, it makes of the shadow*
> *a crown.*

so we draw an image for the individual soul:
a yellow quiet light

> *that softens the edges of sharpest night—*

In Honor of Xipe

Xipe Totec, Aztec god of Spring

I

Slicked

with a birther's goo, it

gleams up green from the ground—

Little blade.

How much toil, to split the sealed doors
of the mother—

And scrape up

through rock and clay, the hard sharp March

of the ground—

our little god, our flayed lord.

—

Xipe Totec (*shee-pay toh-tek*) appears in Aztec art as a human
figure wearing a tunic of human skin.

The hand-skins flop prominently below his elbows, and his
human face, usually grinning, peers out through the eye-slits
and mouth-hole of a skinned-face mask.

He was a god of transitions, oppositions.

After which the rotting skin was removed, and a "new" human being appeared.

—

—in the shimmer,
        their hummingbird cloaks, their

plumed heads
        as they ran toward slaughter—flowers

        in riot on a field—

They flayed the slain captives' skins and wore them, dyed
        "golden clothes"—to impersonate Spring's

        Skinless Lord—

conjure a power I wanted. You know,

to make the corn stand up. Piercing the hardpan
        inside my head, new self

—

        green and scored—

Died. My sister died. In the fourth year
        of parentless night.

Aztec blood-drinking, why should I oppose it? Or put down
      my proper

—

      terror of the earth—

2

They each of them lived in an eating world. Members
      of the Wheel of Mouths—

Owned implements of autosacrifice: a thorn, a carved
      bone,

it was a sacred gift,
      to pierce the soft tissue, feed the earth

      as the earth fed you—

And so gain power
      over the killing-wheel: *not you, not you,* the gods

      in chorus—

When my sister died, after my parents died;

when my sister died; "—stalking your family like a serial killer,"
      someone said;

"Death *is* a serial killer," I had said, when my sister died—

—

It was called Tlacaxipehualiztli, which means "Skinning of Men," and was the first feast of the year within the number of their calendar, celebrated every twenty days...

...and the festival of Tlacaxipehualiztli, before the time of sowing...

...who have studied this divinity and his strange ceremonial and concluded...

...an agricultural rite in which the skin of the victim represented the husk of an ear of corn about to ripen...

...like Prosperpine [*sic*]...

—

Plants change with the conditions.

For the sun their lifting
        cotyledons.

Light being
        at home in their bodies—and the way they

        turn from the dark

when brought in to winter. Half dying, half spreading
        their green hands:

        DAY, DAY, DAY—

And when the priest thrust up the still-steaming heart,
the crowd lifted ears of corn.

Saying, Thy precious water hath come down from Coapan.
It hath made the cypress a quetzal.

Plants

converting light by a windowsill.

—

I was tending them. Those Xipes, Spring's
excruciates—

Easing the blinds
to bend the sun into their green city.

Onto transcripts of birdsong,
gods of rain and war.

To *loved/was loved,* an alien power, under which
(decreed)

all would thrive—

Shocked
into green.

Her Dream

We were arguing about children.
I was pleading,
    "Something could be done, stars could be fixed
    above their hands—"

And then a star-shaped pattern of skin
in a surgical basin.

To be fixed
    to every child's face, ironed over it

    like a wrapper.

Judd Boxes

Marfa, Texas

a book on the Louvre
and a cigarette box

a room without them
was peace

them: meaning   anyone else

—

sometimes, like they were made out of water
sometimes, like they were made out of light
boxes   with their sides disappearing

—

with their insides rippling
triangle pillows

on the couch in squares
where you could
be without speaking

—

childhood living room

—

how like other souls you had
made the choice, but

shape without you
is clean

in the country of aesthetics
where you stand stock-still, trying

—

not to breathe—

no solace in people
but in things

THEREFORE DIRECT YOUR FEELINGS, SENSES, REASON, THOUGHTS UPON THIS STONE ALONE

On stakes, on sticks, one rusted
        bayonet,
left then right, like someone had

planted a packet of hacked-off thumbs
        and the five-fingered harvest
was in—

Left then right.
        "—like I stood in a garden of *hands*—"

                    —

He was alone. He'd stepped off for a piss, it was
        a *secured zone,*
he could smell the far char of the gasolined trees—
        Hands up,

the jungle said.
        And the host won't stop nodding his

                    —

        bashed-in head—

War Vet,
        cable call-in show. You hadn't really been watching,

half-reading a book:

      on alchemy and its Philosopher's Egg,

      now cracked on the jungle floor—

Hands *unless*

      one binds me with measure and a soldier's gun-smashed skull.

      —

And some called it the Copper Stone
      or the Armenian stone; others
the brain stone;
      others the stone which is
no stone; others
      the Egyptian stone;
        and others again the image of the world—

SUN SUTRA

—as if dusk were a page
turning in a book
      and after the bright tale of day with its heroic light

        the quiet story of the stars—

        teaching you their habit
            of jeweling the interior—

so that night
      might not mean loss?

        the art of matter
            is limit and splendor.

This from That

Aurelian,
       who studies the emergence of butterflies
from chrysalides,
       of fighter jets
from number charts,
       of syllables
from kettledrums—

       —

       Insects that pupate in a cocoon
must escape from it
       says Wikipedia.

       Wikipedia, which says:
Whilst inside the pupa

       Says: *digestive juices, to destroy much*
of the larva's body

       larva meaning
its own—

       which has been instructed
to *leave a few cells intact* for

       holometabolous
total change,
       through the nutrients of suffering, of the self-

       carnivore—

(lumbering up,

       hoisting my flesh from the floor—)

—

I study ziggurats
       from cigarettes. *Smoke*

the *effluvium of fire,* the
       fire in the mouth from

cigarettes, from
       ziggurat

       striking dry tinder from the tongue—

"It is queer to be assisting
       at the *éclosion*

—

       of a great new mental epoch,"
wrote William James
       in 1906:

eclosion, verb *eclose,*
       "emergence from concealment"—

which is what "religion and philosophy" do,
       which is what certain

insects do,

    even people, slipping their suits, and what we need

    is a new mental epoch—

whatever lies
    beyond

    self-liquidation—

      —

Aurelian.
    Who studies

    concerto notes
from finger-scales,
    survivor guilt
from firestorms,
    apologies
from bombing runs—

    Through the open back door,
bending a petunia,

Papilio machaon
    drinking deeply

    and long.

SIBYLLINE

Who would
        cast your jaw, after it's broken?

After he speaks in you,
        after you get a little jism from the god—

        —

She *tries to pitch him from her breast,* he *tires out her raving mouth,* it
        shapes by crushing force—

Book VI,
        The Aeneid. The way light comes

        as violation—

in Apollo's black crag
        where his sibyl has to eat it and hum.

        —

Until a chorus comes roaring out of her
        single mouth: *Wars,*

horrendous wars, and blood in the Tiber
        foaming—

Drugged sleep.
        In which I

—

hauled up out of the ocean and strode across the sand,
      dropping clothes as I went—

Five whales! Their barnacled backs
      cresting up

      out of the water—

I had a purpose
      toward what was I striding, dream split

by dawn's fingernail,
      then smashed by that zealot

—

     Noon—

which is what a god can offer
      a petitioning crowd

that is crying,
      I want to wake up, I don't want to wake up—

      —wake up wake up—

Come to me and step behind me,
      put your thumbs gently to the back of my neck—

Make my mouth move—

O voice of a different timbre—

—

You will end up in the street, like you always thought.
Long life, good health, only problems with children.
Something red and an exchange of pesos.
You will not end up in the street.

You will personally feel the crisis of the nation.
You will find love in another city, you will never go back.
You will get the role of "Ham" in the pork commercial.
All your life you will look for a map,

then a padlock will confront you—

ZOZO-JI

Buddhist temple, Tokyo

       One cry from a lone bird over a misted river
is the expression of grief,
          in Japanese. Let women
do what they need.
        And afterward knit a red cap, pray—

In long rows, stone children in bibs and hats, the smell of pine and
          cooled earth—

It was a temple
        for the babied dead. I found it via the Internet.

Where they offered pinwheels
        and bags of sweets
for the aborted ones, or ones who'd lived
        but not enough...

Moss-smell, I can project there.

Azaleas
       pinking the water.

When her lord asked her again how it died, she said
       As an echo off the cliffs of Kegon.

      —

ukiyo: in Japanese it sounds like "Sorrowful World"

winds trying to hold each other
        in silken robes

what in English sounds like "Floating World"

a joke on the six realms in which we tarry

what they called the "Sorrowful World":
        wheel made of winds

trying to cling to each other

        —

        A child didn't jell until the age of seven,
in his body.
        Was *mizuko,* water-child, what in English sounds like
"don't understand"...
        He was a form of liquid life, he committed

        slowly to the flesh—

and if he died or gestation stopped, he was offered
        a juice box and incense sticks, apology and Hello Kitty...

In Japanese, souls spin red-'n'-pink
        rebirth wheels: whole groves *whrrrr-tik-tik* behind the temple

        at Zozo-ji...

—

Sad World. Pleasure World. In some minds
       they sounded the same—

It was a grief aesthetic.

Imagining
       another lit visitor considering a tour,
before finding that it
       needs to start over—

Over the misted river.

Where a banner hangs, saying,
       You Are The 10,056th Person To Visit This Site

and you are the You
       who keeps disembarking.

White Tara

Tibetan, Mother of Compassion

I

With a pillow and a yen.

You were meant to be the god.

Brown eye crowning in its
     jellied boat

        through the unlined winter of your hand.

—

But to view her, not become her.

To have her be your personal god—

Divine bandage
     for each of your wounds, impersonal mother

you could love and love
     and not have to give a thing back—

White Tara. Heart uncurling from the snow of her chest,
     turning blue

     in the Himalayan air—

You bought it in a store.
>After the mother had dropped completely

—

dead—

Facedown
>in a pool of spit, heart's

>fist—

She made you put the gift boots
>back in the box, she said *How*

could you do this to me? when you had to tell her you'd got
>the clap—

Smotherer, eating up all the breath—

She kneels, bearing a heart attack.

—

And the poets say,

>You will not say Mother, you will not say Father—

>We have overthrown
>>the chromosome, we have

>>emerged full-throated from a void.

2

Build it from rot.

From the moldered soil
        of the neglected shit-strewn yard—

Crap-box
        for the neighbor's cats, they love the smell: *alive alive*—

Out of elm sticks
        from the weedy trees, crush and glitter
of yellowed leaves, you must
        build it—
jamb and sill, a frame
        through which she can come

and be the god on the bedroom wall, White
        Lotus—

Seven eyes on the suffering world, still
        in the clothes she was wearing when she

        —

        smacked face-first to the floor—

Rescuing Mother, the poets say.
        Who for.

3

And the poets say,

> You may not admit to bone or flesh, you must not have nerves
> > in the tips of your fingers—
>
> You may say *fist*, you may say *teeth*, but you must not
> > put them in a sentence
> together, you must not put them
> > in a body

—

> together—

in the cemetery
> you pour through the loam.

To find the cold well, its lip lit
> by an oil squeezed

from her bones—*Wrong-Bodied Never*
> *Accomplished Enough* a dose

in the inner ear, how could she
> be the murderer

> when the murderer is in the mirror—

—

In a skin of milk, a moon-warmth white and cool.

You furl out a parentless hand.

To cup the head of the one
        who's been calling you:

                I hated her and then she died—

                she died and then I

                couldn't tell her it was all a lie—

Blood beading the perimeter
        of an almond-shaped wound

        as the eye of compassion slits through.

BARDO

You don't have to break it. Just give it a little
tap.

tap tap. See,

there's the crack. And if you pry it a little
       with the flat end of that spoon,

you'll be able to slip yourself through.

—

To the woods where you're walking. Crushed ice above you
       like a layer of sky—

Some sun under it making it gleam.

Some snow under it bloodless and bright

in the fissured heart, the winter morgue of its imagined
       land.

—

Where you can find her—

Sprawled, facedown, in the snow—

Bracing herself up, a puff of ice at her chin, then seizing
       and dying all over again—

Automaton. You prop her up.

And it's like shaking a doll, *How dare it, How dare it*—

What

        —

good is she for, there in her dying machine?

You push her shoulders back against the trunk of the tree,
        her chest's so cold it cracks—

so you can slip yourself through.
        To the woods she's been walking,

        wondering where the living have gone.

Spring

Forensic Anthropology Center, University of Tennessee, Knoxville

1

The sun, in shafts and spades.

Through the pine and birches, little breeze setting off
        the leaves—

Their golden green increase.

Pollen to the air, its colonial dream
        of a new imperium of trees—

Snap against the wrist-skin.

And then you press down on the tongue with your gloved thumb
        to let the honeybee show you the way.

2

The dark tunnel paths from light to light.

Flay the face and scoop out the eyes—you'll see.

3

Bees in a cloud round your hand.

Egg-herder, your smell
            synonymous with treasure—

Shining a light at the back of the throat:
            blowflies
in liquid pearls
            the bees murder to eat—

And all at the lips and nose a yellow dust, pollen
            they have
delivered—

You scrape it into a little sack.

4

Ripple and snap.

Bend to the O of the rigored mouth—listen:

Plastic bags, like souls, caught in trees.

5

What to harvest
      from the sloughed-off suits of the dead.

Like seashells cupping the ghost-tongue of the sea,
      their black mouths speak—

You crouch to the hum with a bag and a blade. You

the god it sways.

Notes

Cathartes Aura

The poem enacts the Tibetan practice of sky burial, or *jhator* (Tibetan): "giving alms to the birds." *Cathartes aura,* "purifier bird" or "golden purifier," is a species of vulture. *Shey* means "eat" (Tibetan); *shunyata,* "emptiness" (Sanskrit).

Pure Land

The title refers to one of the afterlife abodes of the buddhas. *Chamisa* is a pungent, yellow-flowering bush native to the Southwest.

Refuge Field

Depicted in Tibetan Buddhist tantric paintings (thangkas) or visualized in meditation, *refuge fields* are visual representations of an adept's lineage of gurus and transmission of teachings: a spiritual family tree.

Eight Great Cemeteries, or Charnel Grounds, were prominent cemeteries of ancient India. Charnel grounds have always been important meditation fields for tantric adepts and monks: to confront impermanence in the raw.

The Water

Thanks to Susannah Tyrrell for the poem's last sentence.

Five Skull Diadem

Rinzai, or Línjì Yìxuán (d. 866), was the founder of the Linji School of Chan Buddhism in China. The slapping episode is recounted in D.T. Suzuki's *Zen and Japanese Culture,* 1959. Text for "Tsong Khapa's Praise of the Inner Yama" is a derivation of same from *Essential Tibetan Buddhism,* Robert A.F. Thurman (translated by the author), 1997. *Tsong Khapa,* or

Je Rinpoche (Precious Master), is one of the central master teachers in the Tibetan Buddhist lineage. He died, with "a demonstration of miracles," in 1419.

Yama, or *Yamantaka* (Death Destroyer), is the yak-headed wrathful embodiment of Manjushri, peaceful buddha of wisdom. A dharmapala, or "protector of the dharma," Yama is part of a host of wrathful beings that "throw back into the shadows the forces of nightmare and madness which always threaten to tear loose and subjugate the human psyche" (Vessantara, *Meeting the Buddhas,* 1993). Wrathful Forms are often portrayed wearing the five-skull diadem of the title.

Text in part two of the poem is derived from *The Circle of Bliss: Buddhist Meditational Art,* exhibition catalogue, Columbus Museum of Art, 2003.

Much gratitude to the curators and education staff of the tremendous Circle of Bliss show at the Los Angeles County Museum of Art, which I visited in October 2003.

In Honor of Xipe

Xipe Totec (Nahuatl): "Our Flayed Lord" (or variations thereof).

Part one, section two of the poem slightly reworks passages from *Aztecs,* exhibition catalogue, Royal Academy of Arts, London, 1992.

Part two, section two of the poem lifts from *Book of the Gods and Rites and the Ancient Calendar,* Fray Diego Duran (1579), translated and edited by Fernando Horcasitas and Doris Heyden, 1971, and *The Flayed God: The Mythology of Mesoamerica,* Roberta H. Markman and Peter T. Markman, 1992.

"Thy precious water hath come down from Coapan. / It hath made the cypress a quetzal." From "Song of Xipe Totec Iouallauan," translated from the Nahuatl by Arthur J.O. Anderson and Charles E. Dibble. Originally published in *General History of the Things of New Spain, Book 2: The Ceremonies,* Bernardino de Sahagún (1577), translated by Anderson and Dibble, 1959.

JUDD BOXES

> One hundred untitled works in mill aluminum, 1982–1986, by Donald Judd.

THEREFORE DIRECT YOUR FEELINGS, SENSES, REASON, THOUGHTS UPON THIS STONE ALONE

> Medieval alchemical texts provided the phrasing of the title and the italicized lines in sections three and four.

THIS FROM THAT

> An *aurelian* is a collector and breeder of insects, especially butterflies and moths. *Papílio machaon* is a species of swallowtail butterfly.

ZOZO-JI

> In Japanese, *ukiyo,* or "Floating World," refers to the aesthetic of fleeting beauty and world impermanence informing urban culture, its pleasures and entertainments, in seventeenth-century Edo, Japan. *Ukiyo* is also a homophone for (and thus, for Floating World denizens, a pun on) "Sorrowful World," the Buddhist earthly plane of death and rebirth. For more on Japanese attitudes toward abortion and beliefs about soul incarnation, see William R. LaFleur's *Liquid Life: Abortion and Buddhism in Japan,* 1992.

WHITE TARA

> Tantric Buddhism employs two kinds of thangka meditation: visualizing the god (relational) and visualizing *oneself* as the god (manifest).

BARDO

> *Bar* (in between) plus *do* (suspended, or thrown) (Tibetan): "the state between" life and death (and rebirth); where, for a time, the consciousness of the dead one wanders.

The Knoxville facility (sometimes called the Body Farm) is the only place in the world where cadaver-insect symbiosis can be observed through all its cycles. Such research is crucial to forensic investigations.

—

MARVIN LEVIN ESTHER LEVIN
(2002)

LAURA LEVIN TERRIS
(2006)

About the Author

Dana Levin was raised in California's Mojave Desert and graduated from Pitzer College and NYU's Graduate Creative Writing Program. Her work has received many honors, including a Rona Jaffe Writers' Award, a Witter Bynner Fellowship from the Library of Congress, a Whiting Writers' Award, and fellowships from the Guggenheim Foundation and the National Endowment for the Arts. She lives in Santa Fe, New Mexico.

Since 1972, Copper Canyon Press has fostered the work of emerging, established, and world-renowned poets for an expanding audience. The Press thrives with the generous patronage of readers, writers, booksellers, librarians, teachers, students, and funders—everyone who shares the belief that poetry is vital to language and living.

Copper Canyon Press gratefully acknowledges board member

JIM WICKWIRE

for his many years of service to poetry and independent publishing.

Major support has been provided by:

Amazon.com

Anonymous

Beroz Ferrell & The Point, LLC

Golden Lasso, LLC

Gull Industries, Inc.
on behalf of William and Ruth True

Lannan Foundation

Rhoady and Jeanne Marie Lee

National Endowment for the Arts

Cynthia Lovelace Sears and Frank Buxton

Washington State Arts Commission

Charles and Barbara Wright

*To learn more about underwriting
Copper Canyon Press titles, please call
360-385-4925 x103*

The type used in this book is Requiem, an old-style serif typeface designed by Jonathan Hoefler in 1992 for *Travel & Leisure* magazine. Book design and composition by Phil Kovacevich. Printed on archival-quality paper at McNaughton & Gunn, Inc.

The Chinese character for poetry is made up of two parts: "word" and "temple." It also serves as pressmark for Copper Canyon Press.